icarus and daedalus

I've walked with the sun

  (he and I are brothers)

look at me, dear Icarus

  I've made it so far

  are you proud?

I've walked with the ocean

  (he and I are lovers)

  and listen, dear father

   you made me those wings

   and I've never stopped forgiving
you.

sometimes, dear son

  I see your tears in the sunspots

  (they're the only places I can
look)

  one day

  I'll come back down.

I'll meet you, dear father

  I'll meet you halfway

  I've learned

the ocean's love has mended my
wings

  so now I can fly again.

I've walked with the sun

  his sunspots brought me back to
you

I've walked with the ocean

  his love brought me back to you.

binary star system

I've heard that there are stars

  that can't live without one
another.

  there's something beautiful about
how

  one cries out to the other as it
dies

  and the other

  can't help but die with it

as if

  its grief has never been meant for
anything other than other people's
dreams

I've always wished on those stars

  be careful, they say

  because

  the bigger the star, the bigger the supernova

  but that's never scared me.

I've always wished on those stars.

snow

I believe

that the angels blessed us this morning

  (what else would you call this snow?)

but I've seen it with Icarus' eyes

  and now I can tell you

  it's not as pure as it looks.

I can see the angels' tears in the snow

  (maybe that's all it is

  or maybe

  when they blessed it

  they couldn't hold their tears in anymore)

have you ever thought

  just maybe

  aurora borealis

  is a fire?

  (I've heard the angels talk

  and seen them singe their wings on it)

and have you ever

prayed for a star?

 I have

  and I've heard its thanks

 whispered in my ear

on a cloudy sunday morning

 (as you know

  that's the best time to see stars-

  it's when they bare their souls to
those who listen)

and if you come now, my dear

  we just might see the aurora

  (I can smell smoke

   and where there's smoke, there's
fire

   and I can hear an angel cry out in
pain).

and I believe

  that the angels blessed this snow

but now

  maybe you'll agree

it's not as pure as it looks.

tears of waterdrops

I've read the tears of the
waterdrops running infinitely
towards nothing

  and their gold wings blinded me

   so that I saw.

(I've always believed that blindness

 is the same thing

 as seeing too much.)

and I've seen my wings

 but I never believed in them

(I've always thought

 that it was best to not believe what you see)

and I've flown

 but I didn't believe

and I've read the tears of the waterdrops running infinitely towards nothing

 and their hopes blinded me

the water has never known hope

 (or so I thought)

but there was gold in their minds

and there was love in their eyes.

and I've seen my wings

 but they never needed me to believe in them

(they carried me around despite my disbelief)

and I've read the tears of the waterdrops running infinitely towards nothing.

morse code

I've been told

 the clouds are sleeping tonight

 there's an eclipse tonight

and the stars cried out in morse code

 but I've never understood it

and I saw a plane fly past

 and just for a second

 I wondered

does anyone miss them?

the stars died years ago

 but I see their gilded wings in the lakes

and the fall leaves

  look like their souls.

and riddle me this

  who's the undertaker of the stars?

  who's the groundkeeper of the
heavens?

this winter

  will the snow look like ashes?

  (I've never known a snowfall to
look like anything else)

and this winter

  will the dead leaves look like
black holes?

  (there's nothing better thing to
take your breath away)

and promise me, my dear

  we'll walk together among the
stars

and

  we'll steal Icarus' wings

  (I've seen them in the lakes).

and

I've been told

  the clouds are sleeping tonight

  there's an eclipse tonight

and the stars cried out in morse
code.

there's a forest out there

I've heard there's a forest out there

  it's weeping

  and there's a new river here

  it's flowing

   call it a fire drill-

   it's trying to escape

but

  I've heard there are other worlds out ther

   and now I can believe it

   -the water's burning here

    (I guess that means it has a soul,

     or maybe I'm just naive).

and

  I've heard there's a mountain out there

   it's broken

   they've always called that an earthquake

but I know better-

  it's broken hearted

  and there's nothing more dangerous-

   I guess now the lava can get out

(misery loves company, they say).

and

  I've heard there's a star out there

   it's dying

   so we'll see it soon

   and we'll watch it

    it'll explode so beautifully

   and we cried

    (time doesn't matter here)

and

  I've heard there's a new forest here

  and it's weeping.

wish upon the rain

there's nothing the stars miss
more than rain.

they wish upon it like we wish on
shooting stars

(it's just as rare up there as
shooting stars are down here)

and they watch

as we fall to the ground

just like the rain

and they'll wish upon us

(even the stars stay up waiting for
11:11).

we'll walk on Saturn's rings-

I've always needed a place to
forget the world.

and they say

Pluto's not a planet

but

we disagree

-she may be able to grant fewer
wishes than Jupiter

but she's still a genie

and she still flies.

and we'll walk on the sun-

we can't be burned if we've
already crossed the river Styx.

but we'll watch

  as we fathom our wishes into
constellations

  burning the stars with our eyes

while they wish

  upon the rain.

break so beautifully

just ask, my dear

  and I'll lend you my wings

(just you wait-

  you'll break them so beautifully

I'll never want them to be whole
again).

but we have stars for eyes

  and not in the metaphorical
sense-

I plucked Ursa Major out of the sky

I took her stars as our eyes

don't worry, you got Polaris

-which one do you think it is?

you've always shined better on your infinite side.

and now

these rivers are our sisters

as we set them alight with our eyes

(we never meant to- we only ever wanted

to show them the world)

but don't forget

there's a fire extinguisher nearby

and we'll watch

perfectly content

while it refuses to move.

but just ask, my dear

and I'll lend you my wings.

galaxies

there's another galaxy out there

that's just as lonely

as ours

I've seen it-

we call it

the place where stars go to die-

I've never seen

(or not seen, to be exact)

so many black holes

just

pulling

pulling

pulling

pulling

me in

until

I thank my lucky stars

that I have no lucky stars

and that

the constellation I made with
these hands

has never

seen the dark of day.

and

I've watched

for years upon years

while my stars orbit each other

and

though they've never

seen the dark of day

they know how intensely nothing it
feels.

and

I thank my lucky stars

that I have no lucky stars

because

there's a galaxy out there

that's just as lonely

as ours.

wishing for winter

there's another galaxy out there

that's just as lonely

as ours

I've seen it-

we call it

the place where stars go to die-

I've never seen

(or not seen, to be exact)

so many black holes

just

pulling

pulling

pulling

pulling

me in

until

I thank my lucky stars

that I have no lucky stars

and that

the constellation I made with these hands

has never

seen the dark of day.

and

I've watched

for years upon years

while my stars orbit each other

and

though they've never

seen the dark of day

they know how intensely nothing it feels.

and

I thank my lucky stars

that I have no lucky stars

because

there's a galaxy out there

that's just as lonely

as ours.

darkness

I've heard

  that the stars love nothing more

  than darkness.

(I suppose if you live your life
making light, you'd have to.)

but I saw the river they made

  (I'm not sure, but I heard their
whispers

  they said it was a hobby of
theirs)

  and it shone so bright

   that

I haven't seen since.

but don't worry, my dear

  it's such an exquisite blindness

  that I wouldn't wish for anything
else.

and

  you won't believe it

  but yesterday

it rained fire

  (I guess the stars were crying)

but

  the trees just stood by and
watched

   and wept

(they felt each others' pain).

and

  a black hole died today.

but

  no one laid flowers on its grave

   (I guess they figured its
loneliness was deserved)

and

no one will read its obituary

(the stars have been censoring the
papers recently).

because

I've heard

the stars

love nothing more

than darkness.

hurricanes

I

am why

they name hurricanes

after people.

I've heard my name in whispers

and my stars

have made the most
beautiful black holes

(how can a black hole be
beautiful? you ask

well

I guess you'll have to wait

for my stars

to go up in flames

and my winds

to braid your hair

so exquisitely

that you will beg for me to come
back).

I

am why

they name hurricanes

after people.

.

but I think there's something beautiful

 about the way that the moon needs the sun to shine

 and the way that the sun lives vicariously through it at night

I went stargazing tonight

 the moon was too bright to see stars

 (replacing silver with brighter silver)

 now watch me take it and make an island

 come with me, my dear

 we'll make an island more beautiful than any we've ever seen

 and

we'll see stars

 and those stars will have children

 and we'll see those stars

(what do you call the opposite of a black hole?

symbiosis

let's call it

 symbiosis

the way we need each other

 like plants need air and air needs plants

 or how a life taken by one is a life taken from all

and call me

 naive

if black holes take all the light,
would it give it all back?)

and

I'll make you wings from the
silver of the island

(call it the tree of flight- I'll plant
a feather in the silver ground

and we'll pluck wings off that
tree)

we'll fly away-

it's only courteous to leave wings
for others, I guess

and we always have been the
courteous types

so come with me, my dear

come to my island of silver

call it whatever you want

but I'll call it

moonlight.

eyes of a cat

I dreamt last night

(truly dreamt- for the first time in
ages

maybe Hermes stole my
dreams)

I saw the world

through the eyes

of a cat.

where love

was unconditional and eternal

my eyes were stars

(but living stars- you can't see
with ten thousand year old eyes)

and I found forgiveness around
every corner.

and

just for a few seconds at a time

I flew.

dear genie,

since I woke up

I have but one wish.

I want to see life

with the eyes of a cat.

connection

there's nothing quite like

connection.

like knowing

that no matter what

my liberation

is intertwined with yours.

that

while there is a soul in prison

I am not free.

and

like knowing

that my stars are yours

and yours mine.

there's nothing quite like

justice.

like saying

that my ears are open

that I will do what I can

because

I cannot be free while you are
oppressed

I cannot fly while society holds
you in chains.

and

like knowing

that while I can fly

it is my job

to break you from these bonds

to free you from your chains.

because

we have a connection

(we're both human- I wish more

of us could see

how incredibly

enough

that is).

because

my liberation is intertwined with
yours.

and while there is a soul in prison

I am not free.

empty space

the cosmos are made

of 90% empty space

and millions of years

of ashes.

and they never tire

"come walk with me,"

says Venus to Mars

(or should I say "said"?

it's been billions of years

but they're still walking.)

the cosmos are made

"walk with me," says the sun

of 90% empty space.

(maybe that's what threw
off

the church?)

the cosmos are made

of 90% empty space

and billions of years of hopes

"dream with me," said Polaris.

(thirty million years ago)

and I just heard it today.

and millions of years of ashes

they made me

eighteen years ago

(the ultimate recycling plant).

an open letter to dell

Dear Dell,

what does obsolesence mean to
you?

 is it the dead wasteland soccer
field where young boys in Ghana
feast on lead for food

 and toxic fumes as air?

 is it the body of the young man
in India

 dead at 19

 whose choice was death for
him or for his children?

 what do you see in the
containers that you send across
that ocean?

 money?

 I see the bodies of young boys
in Ghana and China

 the bodies of boys working to
death so they can live

and

what does "away" mean to you?

 you throw their lives away

 as if they were just some
outdated piece of electronic waste

 or does it mean profit?

 does it mean that they're worth
more dead than alive?

"externalizing the cost".

what does that mean?

 it means that playing in a deadly
soccer field is a fact of life

 it means that we're going to have
to change wikipedia

 "human: a species fallen victim
to its own greed

 who defines life in
dollars

 diet: a piecewise
function

 extravagencies for
the rich

 and their trash for
the rest of us."

and

it means

we all have blood on our hands

and in our waste.

conveniently left

 in a place called "away".

somewhere

 just around the corner from the
milky way

(greetings from your galactical
next-door neighbors)

 you were mourning

 for some star you loved

 (I know what we call it- β UMi

 but what was its real name?

   what constellation did its soul
go by?)

but somehow

 you still showed me the way

 (was it distance that kept you from
the supernova? caring? self-
preservation?)

I guess

 I could say

you taught me what selflessness is

 (four hundred light years away

dear polaris

dear polaris

   I found you last year

and still you give us your light-

I guess I could learn a thing or two
about sharing from you)

can you tell me a little something
about your friends?

what's it like needing your two
companions so profoundly?

do you fear the supernovae?

 (you'll be one someday)

then again

 never forget,

 dear polaris,

 you make up everything

(you're the mortar to the galaxy's
bricks)

will you remember me, dear
polaris?

 I remember you

dear polaris

 I found you last year

I hope someday you find me.

what I'm made of

 like Icarus

 I've heard we're made of dead
stars

(when you die, dear Icarus,

remember me in your will?)

some inheritance of compassion

it's something left over from long-gone ages

or birthright of love

 like Pythagorus, some old Greek's magic formula

and 35% wind

65% oxygen?

 (it stiched the feathers in my wings together-

 (I feel bad for the last 1%- no one to bind to

the wind felt golden on my back)

it's no wonder O3 is so unstable)

like Icarus

last night,

 I'm made of fourteen billion years of dreams.

 I saw a star implode from too much caring

 I'd like to think I'm made from stars like that

borrowed wings

I stole these wings from someone

I can't remember who- just

look in my eyes and they'll tell you

but you won't take them from me

I've stitched them on my back
with the thread of dreams

(we're all made of dreams, I
guess, in a way

but this thread can't be broken
with diamonds.)

I've always thought that there's
something beautiful

in how a forest needs fire to live

and I've never found beauty except
when I watched the dawn

(let me define beauty to you-

it's watching the rebirth of
something

watching it overcome hardship

like birds who would never fly
unless they were pushed out of
their nest)

and I just remembered

it was gravity that gave me these
wings

(I still don't know why)

but I won't give them back

I'll stitch them ever tighter to my
back

and the flames will cement the
thread

while I fly over the burning forest

(and the flames won't bring me
down)

the wind in the clouds

the wind won't stop screaming

I heard it in the clouds last night

(I was walking among them

next to the stars

hitchhiking rides on planes)

but not a one ever stopped for me

(the fire was too close-

there's danger in the clouds too)

the sun was like a shark

it could taste blood from 93,000,000 miles away

and there's a feeding frenzy in the cosmos

and the stars laughed while the sky burned

and not a one person stopped

no one stopped for me

or the stars.

and the wind wouldn't stop screaming.

ursa major

I've been told

you can see the stars perfectly on cloudy days

that ursa major likes to tuck her little child in with cloud covers

and pisces likes to swim in their muddy bright waters.

but I swear that cloud is just another name for smoke

I saw a forest fire not ten yards away from those stars

and who would have known that a fish out of water would burn so well?

there's a funeral in the cosmos tonight

(but how can you bury a star that's been dead for centuries?)

and there's a forest crying out in exquisite agony

it knows it's better off with a new start

and its smoke helped to tuck in a baby bear.

I've never seen the stars so well from the city

I guess that even the light pollution has to take nights off

though I've never really known if I was really seeing the stars

or if I was just in a giant planetarium

and I forgot to turn off the clouds.

I've heard that the ocean ran away with the stars

so I guess that would explain why there's no reflection of them

though I admit I've always favoured the fanciful

and I've slept with ursa minor on a cloudy day

tucked him in under his mother's watchful eye.

I walked ten miles away

and I pulled the blanket off a sleeping bear.

I've always seen the stars much better on sunny days.

inside the milky way

There's a star in our galaxy that
lost everything

 it's weeping, and here they call
that solar wind

maybe that's what the milky way
really is-

 I've learned that there's nothing
more beautiful than a tragedy.

 (I guess Lear must've thought that
too).

and I watched from the lake as it
happened

 (I know we can't see it yet, but
that's a technicality

  I felt the shockwaves ten years
ago).

 and I've stood on the sometimes
not frozen lake for countless
supernovas

(the probabilities say so, at least)

 but I've never known.

and they'll see it in another million
years or so

 I guess our night sky is just a
graveyard

 maybe that's why all the stars are
named after dead gods

(you remember that gods can die
just like stars).

though nothing ever dies while
people still talk about it.

and the birds never stop flying till
the atmosphere is gone.

and the fire doesn't stop burning
till it can't breath.

I guess that's the problem with the
milky way

-should we make a name for it?
tragedy is always the most
beautiful.

 it'll never go away till it dies

and it will

will you come to the funeral with
me?

 wait at that corner-

  there's a stoplight there

  it won't turn green till a black
hole forms

 (but Stephen Hawking says we
can jaywalk).

come with me

 remember

there's a star in our galaxy that lost
everything.

skydiving

you told me

  the stars watched over me that
day

but I was flying at midday

  and I swear I could only see the
moon at sunrise

but flying has never come easily
for me

  (though I guess you could say
these golden wings have always
known how)

and I've always had trouble
remembering that the sun always
rises

  (the rainclouds have always tried
to trick me)

I've always loved how the birds
learn to fly

  you never know you can fly until
you have no other choice

  and my wings have come to love
falling out of the nest

  so I guess skydiving has always
been a love of mine

  (after all, what is skydiving but
falling from safety to freedom?)

the winds always carry me when I
fly

  it has nothing to do with the tide,
the scientists tell me

  but I only fly under a full moon

  (the light of day has always
scared me

  and who is truly not afraid of
the dark?)

and yes, the stars were watching
over me then

  though who's to say if it was day
or night?

  my wings were straddling
midnight and noon.

and I've always loved how the
birds learn to fly

  I guess you could say that's how I
found freedom too.

I fell out of my nest

  and it was a full moon

and the winds carried me away
from safety to freedom.

lamplighters

have you ever thought that the
stars need polishing?

(I can promise you it was Icarus'
last thought).

but I've never trusted the
lamplighters

 -the soul of fire is contagious

 and it has wings just like mine.

hold your head up, they whisper to
the burning buildings

though I guess even the flames
need to breathe

and even my wings need to be
stretched every so often

(these wings are strongest when
stretched).

so come with me, my dear

come walk among the stars

(I guess you could call us
gravediggers, but we just clean the
headstones).

hold your hands over the
lamplighters' fires

you'll leave a trace in the sky

(how many people get to see their
epitaphs before they die?)

but even forever has to end

so carve it with fire, not with
diamond

(best make it easier for the next
polishers of the sky).

the streetlights have never seemed
that tall to me

  but they must be-

  these lamplighters' shadows are
forever

(Icarus burned his wings trying to
change the bulb).

have you seen the dead souls up
here?

 I guess souls are like moths

  -they love to die in the light

but have you ever thought the stars
need polishing?

don't trust the lamplighters

  we'll do it ourselves

(it's our job to clean off the
headstones of the stars).

and don't forget Icarus' last words

so come polish the stars with me

  dip your hand in the fire

and watch with me as the eternal
ends.

and the sky is growing smoky

(all the better to hide in)

just talk to it, my dear

pray to the flames

they'll set you right on the clouds

(I've always wanted to live up here)

and just you wait, my dear

stars for rainy days

run

Daedalus will be so jealous of this place

but I've never been afraid of fire

its wings and mine are brothers-

and Icarus will never fly this high

(our souls will melt his wings)

freedom is all either of us has ever wanted

could you spare some gold, my dear?

just start talking-

open your heart to me and I'll take
it from there

we'll line the clouds with it

  silver linings will be nothing
compared to what they'll see in our
clouds

we'll make stars out of them

  (save them for rainy days

  they'll coax the sun out of
hiding)

so, my dear,

  promise me you'll be there when
the smoke clears?

I need this fire to make our stars:

  one part your words, one part
clouds, one part stardust

we'll write our names in the sky

lace these woods with gold

and brighten the night sky.

but save your words, my dear

  (save them for a rainy day)

this fire will hug you so tightly

  (your soul will be so beautifully
charred)

but don't run

  it will only fan the flames.

and, dear Icarus,

  come meet your father

  he's up in the clouds

(where you could never be-

if you just talk to the flames,
they'll protect you).

stars were gone last night, I had
taken them all

he's making stars with us

I used their light to write on your
arms

and saving them for rainy days.

but it's like that childish game we
used to play

don't look

you'll spoil the surprise

you'll break the spell

it's a secret, I say

to make a black hole

you don't say anything

will you teach me how to make a
black hole?

we took the gold from the sun, call
us thieves if you want

*well, you made one last night, or
don't you remember the*

I prefer Robin Hood-

the sun already has enough
beauty, and the fire will burn
without its gold

giving them to Icarus seemed like
a betrayal at the time

  (we're fortune tellers here- we
knew what would happen)

  but we did it anyways

  and Daedelus' cries drew no pity
from us

you can never come back from
your freedom.

I've always found it curious that
Icarus has no constellation

  (the night sky envies those who
steal its thunder)

but yes, it's true

  we made a black hole last night.

you look at your arm for a second

  and for a second, you know
exactly what it says

and then

you know you broke the spell

all doubt vanishes an instant later-

  the stars are back in the sky

and just for a second

  you see Icarus flying on stolen
wings

but then the second is over

the sun has its gold back

our childish game is over

and we've forgotten

how to make a black hole.

and I haven't flown in ages

(do I still have my wings?)

but come with me, my dear

come climb a mountain

and we'll coax the sun out

(who can resist your honey-sweet voice?)

and we'll shout it from the mountaintops

(I know there are none around-
we'll build one with our love).

and to me, infinity has never meant anything

but a broken promise

and a starry sky

golden wings

it's been windy for weeks now

but even the stars are broken
promises-

  they lie with their very existance.

three million meters per second-

  but we'll just call it a broken
promise.

so just climb on my back, my dear,

  we'll fly up to the stars

come count them with me-

  every star is a broken promise

  that we can use to make a river of
our dreams.

and we'll never sell that river

  even though we could make
millions

  (our dreams are made of gold)

and I'll sit alone with you at 1 am

by the banks of the river

and we'll swim together,

coating my wings with gold.

and I'll never doubt that I have
wings

and I'll never be like Icarus-

  no golden sun can melt my
golden wings

and once we've coaxed the sun to
bed

  climb on my wings

and we'll count the broken
promises

  and make them into stars

and then we'll be

  infinite.

forest of my mind

you told me yesterday.

  you hugged me from behind

while you said

  that you knew how I felt,

that you knew that minds could be
terrifying places.

and I know that you know

wandering through the forest of
my mind,

  I swear that I've seen you flying

(forgive me- I've never been one to
fantasize

  I've seen too much of Icarus to
believe that people can fly).

and somehow

  your presence comforted me

(I could feel it, even though I
didn't believe-

    feeling is believing, not seeing).

but it was a hot summer

  so come, watch while the forest
burns

(don't fly too high- you'll burn
your wings

don't fly too low- you'll burn your
soul).

and if you ever fall

  remember me when you hit the
ground.

  remember what I told you while
you lie on the cold soil

  feel the grass on your cheek and
think of the sun.

and remember

  it'll be winter soon,

  the birds will fly to the warmth-

    (but they'll leave their souls here-

    they stick to everything they
touch).

promise me, dear Icarus,

you'll watch as they cut down that
forest.

or maybe

might you even weep?

  I've seen fires put out by less.

or maybe

  it might even stop them

  (they don't know what they're
doing anyways.)

but, my dear,

my mind is a terrifying place.

and don't fly too low

 lest that forest burn your soul.

reach for the

I've never been able to catch you

you've always lived among the
stars

   and I've never known the
password to climb above the
clouds.

reach for the stars, they say

   and then they tie my hands down.

I've never believed that words can't
hurt

   just look down and these ropes

my bonds are made of their
words and they're stronger than

because

-than infinity

your words have cut my soul

but infinity's a curse word here,
everything ends

like breadcrumbs I leave pieces
of it whenever I speak

(the stars would have you believe
otherwise)

so just take those shreds of paper,
my dear

so will you just take off these
bonds?

give them to me

I'll heal the tears in my broken
soul

let me walk with them

they'll never call me Jonah once I
face my fears

burn those pages that ground me
here like lead

(I'll never walk again otherwise)

and we'll believe in infinity

even though it's a swear word

and this prison will be nothing but
a memory

they'll call me Jonah, I'll run
away

and we'll taste it on our lips

while we watch the infinite end.

but I'll never be lost to you.

they could feel the warmth still

(they were all partly inside me

and once they died, they could
feel my pain)

flames like a cat

there were flames lapping at these
pages last night

(just like a cat-

they can't see what isn't always
there

they have to feel for life inside my
soul)

and my heart wept while these
pages burned

but still

the old paper smelled so sweet in
its dying hour

and I head the stars cry

they wept as my soul burned

but, my dear, I am made of
stardust

(or so you told me- and some
days I believe you)

but it's been years since then

(years since this snow fell, and
it's still here)

it's winter deep inside my soul

and I remember

I burnt those pages long ago

(I lit the fire for warmth-

but it feels like it took its warmth
from my soul

and it's been winter ever since)

and it's winter deep inside my soul

  it seems even stardust can go cold

(after all, it's always cold in space:

I heard the average temperature is
22 degrees

below consciousness)

but today it's absolute zero in my
heart

and now

just watch me, my dear

I'll set fire to these heartless pages

  and watch

as the flames lap at them like
thirsty cats

feeling

to see inside my soul.

and soon

these flames will warm me up

and I can promise

one day

once I've set fire to these heartless
pages

I'll be made of stardust once again.

falling

  falling

    falling

    falling

and I could barely stand up.

my cheek hit the ancient ground

and its five billion years felt new
against my lips

falling

and this water wouldn't wake up in
the morning.

I swear that this weight didn't hug
my leg last night

but then again, I do remember

but this grass smiled at me with the
innocence of a newborn baby

 in my dreams

 (it is newborn- there was only
despair here when I last saw it)

 I was flying

and then

and it cried when the morning
came

 but I like to think that those tears

might have been tears of joy

(it survived the long night-

  the cold only made it more
colourful).

and there'll be fire soon, we're long
overdue

 the ground told me that it misses
the warmth

the hot scorching torture of it

the almost cold heat of a new era

the beautiful warmth of rebirth

the hopelessness of the drought

and the fire was beautiful last night

 (who ever knew that I would be
one to smile

 while five billion years burned in
less than a minute)

but I still couldn't walk

I looked down at my leg

  watching while it burned

  (the forest that I built)

and in the weight that hugged my
leg

I saw a reflection

and I watched

as it

(as I)

flew on the ground

and as I fell

 falling

  falling

  falling

while the ancient ground burned.

because

(I swear to you, my dear)

  the sea looks just like heaven

  and these fish look just like stars

there's a shooting star, make a wish

  (or is that Icarus? these falling
dreams all look the same to me)

and these eyes all shine down on
me

 but I can't tell if they're laughing
or crying.

So open your eyes, my dear

  it's daytime now, wake up

  don't be afraid- the monsters are
all gone

  (or not- they're all in my mind)

have you seen?

  let me open that door-

  I know there are skeletons in
your closet,

   some of them are mine-

so I guess there are monsters in the
daytime too.

as the water laughs

 look up at the stars, you told me

   they shine for you.

but this water laughed when you
said that

and this boat cried to hear that
sound

Open your eyes- it's daytime now,
but darkness is infinite

   but you'll chase it away-

   infinity can have an end if you
want.

darkness will come back,

so keep opening your eyes, you'll
chase it away

(but not too fast- I want to see the
stars)

and I'll go dwn to the shoreline

and cry

as the water laughs.

nothing so beautiful

 Have you ever seen a river burst
into flames at the end of a star?

   I have

and I promise you

  there's no death more beautiful
than the death of the infinite.

the vultures have long since
stopped circling

   (if there's no end to something,
they can't devour it when it ends)

and here

the water sparkles like remains of
dead stars

(that's what it is-

it's that precious)

and the planets have long since
circling the sun mockingly

(today, they have no energy left
to orbit-

the vultures have found them)

and here

the fire burns your soul like a
mocking match

a fire when you want nothing
more than to be cold

and ice when all you could ever
want is warmth.

but you've done this to yourself,

you say

even though

you know that infinity did this to
you

because

you've sworn it a thousand times

even the infinite has to end

those vultures are made of
stardust too

and they need sustenance as
well.

but stars don't burn, you say

have you seen the smoke in the
air on cloudy nights?

you know, my dear

where there's smoke, there's fire

and it goes on endlessly

without end until it stops.

and you told me

you wanted to swim

so step in that river

and let the stardust wash over you

and engulf you endlessly

while the vultures circle above

waiting for the endless to end.

And then the fire spread

I watched as it devoured the forest that we'd built

the trees we'd crafted with these hands

walk among the stars

And the stars came out today

the leaves we'd made with our tears

I walked down to the lake and I saw them

the grass we'd grown with our breath.

the lake burned while I watched

(I've never seen water burn before either, my dear

And I walked through the burning forest

but just trust me)

and I heard you whisper to me through the trees

but they answered before I could
hear what you'd said.

when this winter ends

(will it? I've lost faith in spring)

And now, my dear

I'll walk down to the ocean

it's been winter for ages

(or lake- just like my dreams,

and every night I go out in the
snow

I can't see the other side).

And I lie in the snow

But every star I've ever met has
cried at night

and watch while the stars mock
me with their endlessness.

they die each night, just like us

and then

so I guess that endlessness does
not mean immortality.

And I spend each day in their cemetery

(you and I are nothing but dead stars)

But I still can't see them from below the clouds

And they'll watch us

as we fall

(we're all just like Icarus in the end)

But this sky is never-ending

and who says that everything has gravity?

I've never actually touched the ground.

But I've felt the ground burning beneath me

(wandering through that burning forest

that we built)

We walk every day among the stars.

And we'll build this forest again

just come with me, my dear

we'll coax the stars down

weightless

and they'll cry their tears into the ground

you told me

I'm made of stardust

and moonlight

but I haven't glittered in ages

all that glitters is not gold

So when we walk through this burning forest

they say

but they can't see it through the clouds

or maybe the clouds hide you from me.

We can say

but it's been raining for ages

and yet I haven't felt it- maybe

the rain has numbed my nerves

or maybe the stars have taken them

but tell them

  I'll come back

  (we all are stardust)

but right now

  I'm on the clouds right now

  (it seems)

but

  tell me,

  if I look down,

will I fall?

or

I've heard that

 we're all made of water

 so does that mean

 that I'm weightless?

but

stardust floats too

so why will I still fall?

maybe

  the moonlight is in love with the ocean floor

I've seen the light coming from the depths

  even in the Marianas trench I can still see

  there's darkness in the light

but give me stardust

I'll make you

  build you

  from the ashes

(two parts stardust, one part moonlight)

you'll be the brightest star anyone's ever seen

and

we'll see you as we walk upon the clouds

and

as they fall to the ground

the pair of us will watch

and we'll be

weightless.

same sky

sometimes I think it's comforting

 that we're all under the same sky

but sometimes I think we have to
shrug this blanket off our
shoulders

because closeness can sometimes
strangle us

but this sky

 is the most beautiful blanket I've
ever seen.

sometimes

 I lie under it at night

 and I like to imagine

 that these little spots that make it
so interesting

 are little holes that someone's
cut out of the blanket

 and someone up above is
shining a light through them.

and

 these negative spaces shrink

 (I thinkI hope)

when you remember

that we're all under this blanket

we're more the same than you
know.

negative space

they say

 the space in between our bodies
makes shapes

 that if you look long and hard
enough,

you might see something of a
long-forgotten past

but I've never been one to look
back

so I keep seeing the future in the black

and sometimes

this gift haunts me

but sometimes

(when the night's clear enough)

I can see stars come between me and them

but

their minds are stuck in the middle ages

when those stars lived

and

while I lie upon this rooftop

the city lights look like paper stars to me

not even dimensional enough to call one-dimensional

so I stare at them

and starting today

this window is a star that lived a million years ago

this flooded street is the milky way

and that traffic light changes

sometimes it's Jupiter

sometimes it's Saturn

and on really good days when my mind can't wander past the street corner where it stands

it gets to be Mars

but those are the rare days

most times I follow each person walking aimlessly purposefully backwards

like comets I know I'll never see them again

but as they fall from earth

I wish upon them like a shooting star

that some day

this space between us

(me and you, dear stranger)

will disappear.

but until then

I'll just lie upon this roof

watching the negative spaces
expand into endless nothingness

watching the flooded street milky
way evaporate until all that you
know is gone

watching the traffic light change
from Jupiter to Saturn and
sometimes to Mars

watching the people go past like
shooting stars

and the constelations between us

will never stop telling me the
future

and I'll never stop reading the
negative spaces.

it hasn't rained

It's been years since I felt the rain
on my face

  but they won't call it a drought-
it's rained since then

and I've rowed in a boat of dreams

  and I wanted to dip my hands
into the sea

  to feel the saltiness of their tears
sting my eyes

  to know I was alive

but the stars would start crying
when I did

  and their tears felt so much more
delicious on my face

(the dead cry so beautifully

  maybe that's why the grass is
always wet in the mornings)

and I've felt the sun cool my heart
on a warm summer day

  even though I never liked air
conditioning

and I looked into their eyes in
midmorning on a starry day

and they twinkled so brightly they
blinded me

and I've been blind

        deaf

        senseless

        unfeeling

ever since.

but don't worry about me, my dear

I see just fine without my eyes

'cause they say insight is 20/20

And this summer

I saw my first forest fire

there was a lake nearby

and I could have sworn the lake
was burning

while the trees laughed
delightedly.

the trees always know how to find
the silver lining in everything

-it's only the silver clouds that cry

  when the trees are too thirsty to
drink

but today

the clouds just watched

and the trees just smiled

while the lake burned.

But I promise you, my dear

it will rain soon

  and we'll feel the stars etch their
stories on our faces

  as the salt water carves the words
into our soft cheeks.

and I'll feel the wet grass on my
bare feet

(the dead cry so beautifully)

and I'll stand

as the sun warms my heart

in the dark december cold

and as it rains

they'll call it a drought

and we'll laugh

as we watch some far-off lake
burn.

but just ask me, my dear, and I'll walk as slowly as the stars on a lazy sunday morning

and I guess you can call me naive

but I've never felt more awake than in my dreams

with no one watching, I can fly so far

prove it, you say

but I get stage fright

or maybe others pull me down

I know that my wings are made of lead

but I still fly

and when you force my wings shut

it only reminds me

that

-I-

can fly

and there is no sadder creature

than a bird

with broken-hearted wings.

lazy sundays

The clouds have never been able to catch me

but without this ache in my back

  I might forget who I am

  (or who I have been- the sky has
no concept of time)

or if you'd show me my path

I'll be sure to wave when I walk
the other way

because

 all you've ever done

  is hurt me

(or show me who I am)

and I know

 I've never thanked you yet

  (but don't hold your breath:

   you never meant to heal

   and I never meant to hurt)

and I've watched you gaze at the
clouds

 on clear monday afternoons

and I've never smiled so
conflictedly

 as those times when I saw you
from the sky

  (could you see me?)

but just watch the clouds

  and if they ever catch me

  and if I ever fall

promise me

  that you won't touch my wings

and if the clouds ever catch me

just tell me, my dear

and I'll walk as slowly as the stars
on a lazy sunday morning.

your wings

you never think about your words

like daggers on delicate flesh they
cut right through me
"Ladies and gentlemen"
it's been years since you've thought
anything of it, you've forgotten
the feel of fire on your cold flesh

the feel of a knife as it cuts
through your wings
grounding you

but not me.
I haven't forgotten
every time you write me away
(if you try so hard to hold me
down,
I'll just fly away)

do you remember
when your wings hurt like daggers
there's a fire ahead,

you can't stay away, the flames
have you in a trance
your words keep fanning them
and you can't stop.

tell me
how hot is that fire?
I can bet you it burns as hot as
your hate
(if you fly over it, you'll melt your
wings
go ahead, try
are you that careless?)

the tides will wash it out
will you see me here, bleeding,
reaching for the sky?
(it's only a few miles away)

tell me
do you see me here

bleeding
every time
you make me choose?

remember that fire.

remember
years ago
when you felt that on your wings.

but now I've seen you soaring
high over Everest
you barely breathe
(you're right, it would break the
spell)
so at least let me climb on your
back
and together
we'll soar far away from hatred

far above Everest.

tides and stars

you say

these tides come and go
these stars come and fade
tell me

will I too?
will my time come soon, will I be
a name
a statistic
a memory barely there
vanishingvanishingvanishingvanis
hed

I won't let the moon control me
I'd sooner
die, you say

that's good, my dear
you'll be gone soon, and
what'll really matter is how you go

close your eyes so peacefully, just
like
(it's not like sleeping, my dear, it's
not)

still close your eyes
take my hand, I won't let us drift
apart
(drifting apart is what other people
do,
not us)

close your eyes and see the stars
(you're so like them- so beautiful,
so bright
so fleeting)

you'll be a memory, I promise
you'll be remembered
like a tide,

come and go

and take the sand
with you.

wishing upon stars

you say

these tides come and go
these stars come and fade
tell me

will I too?
will my time come soon, will I be
a name
a statistic
a memory barely there
vanishingvanishingvanishingvanis
hed

I won't let the moon control me
I'd sooner
die, you say

that's good, my dear
you'll be gone soon, and
what'll really matter is how you go

close your eyes so peacefully, just
like
(it's not like sleeping, my dear, it's
not)

still close your eyes
take my hand, I won't let us drift
apart
(drifting apart is what other people
do,
not us)

close your eyes and see the stars
(you're so like them- so beautiful,

so bright
so fleeting)

you'll be a memory, I promise
you'll be remembered
like a tide,

come and go

and take the sand
with you.

to philadelphia

so I guess the field of brotherly
love has an outside border
    it's the berlin wall again, the US
has an east Germany
        and we call it the slum

it's a prison they're born into
        there's no escape

and its inmates call it home.

tell me, do you close your eyes
when you drive by the dilapidated
buildings?
have you seen an accident caused
by blindness?
        because that's what this place

is.   ◦

I guess it's a necessary evil, a side
effect of a medication that hasn't
yet worn off

but wishing doesn't make it so
they won't go away

slums are the measure of
civilization
so what does that tell you about
ours?

so be my guest, my friend
close your eyes to their suffering
    (you're blind to everyone else's,
anyways)

but remember
it could have been you in that
prison,
sentenced to life for a crime that
never happened

and would you call it home?

I saw a spectre wading in a far off
river

it was carrying a spade, wearied
but not from staying up far past its
bedtime
not from waiting for its time to
shine
not from staying up long nights
and longer days, reading until its
eyes stopped opening after a blink

but weary from digging its own
grave
weary from days when it wasn't
there,
(because if you're not seen, you're
not there

or so I've heard)

and now the air's thinning

we're flying so high now
and we thought we'd see
everything
but we (and I mean to say you)

see

nothing

a spectre

no buildings, no one
and you're crying now
because
-you say-
what if
what if what you can't see is what's
not there?

what if
what if this whole world isn't
there?

what if this whole world

is just a spectre

wading in a far off river
with a shovel on its shoulder

digging its own grave?

there's a man on the sidewalk

there's a man on the sidewalk

you can see he's

dying

flying   but you lost it in the routine, like
                                              balsa wood the wings snap

the blood covers everything, like
                                              and there's red all over, you can
snow on a white christmas   see you're

you've never seen so much red

                                              flying

like a blur, you walk past   dying

                                              crying

                                              the bloody tears sting your eyes,
                                              you've never known this much
as your thoughts fly away after   pain
him

(on Icarus' wings)
                                              and now your eyes are so red, the
                                              blood flows down your face like

I can tell that they're looking for
him
                                              tears for a lost soul
they're looking for you, for your
soul

and down into the storm drain,
they say that

every single one of them is

things like this, they spread

flying

and with all the vaccines that we
have, our immune systems have

sinking

crying

never been weaker,

and the crowd walks past

dying too.

they can see you're

flying

dying

crying

blind

and now I can't see

and inside

you say it's

blindness   waiting

that it's the mardi gras masks that   waiting for the dark
hide your true self

                                                   and if you wake up, I promise you

but I see your glass heart beating
(let me crack it-I promise I'll do it
so carefully)   I promise you I'll be there.

and we're made of glass-you see
right through me, all the way to   because whatever they may say, I
my plastic center   can hear your heart beat

                                               and it shines so brightly, I can see
                                               through all the masks

but I'm afraid of the dark

there's nowhere to hide from all
the vultures that tear your heart out   and the vultures will still circle

                                               but it's proven, they can't see glass

and they're circling overhead now,
waiting   so I guess you're

waiting

it's our new sight that will open
their eyes

safe-I'll watch over you, keep you
warm

and in a world where everyone is
blind

(glass is like ice: it freezes, just
like your heart)

we'll rise from the ashes

I'll keep you alive- they only feed
on the dead anyways

and with our one eye, we'll show
them the truth

and as we wait for the next
carnival

so just take off your mask, my
dear-

get out your mask-not like you
ever put it away

(how can you see when your
reflection is a lie?)

what's your real face now?

we'll shoo the vultures away

but we'll see-

and we'll be their leaders

cut eyeholes in the masks with the
darkness

and we'll never be

when they say that we're blind

afraid

we'll pass their tests- bottom row,
third letter: that's a trick, I promise
you even their tests feed us more
lies

of our true selves

of the dark.

every second, boom, boom, boom

if could've seen, it's only blood
that you would've seen

to war's unknowns

no one would remember you, you
knew from the start

so why did you join?

you always felt the fire, the heat on
your skin

always the heat

your mother died of pain

and you died in vain

you condemned war

you were judge and prosecutor at
the same time

you've never seen anything-

  you were blind from birth

  but it escaped, and now comes
the despair

and the realization

but despite that, you went to war

(head held high, a ready target
waiting to be shot)

that you

-you died in vain

you didn't see where you were
shooting, but still you shot

and no one will remember you.

like parallel bars, they swing
between us

(the world does, and we just

    watch while they

sit idly with their hands as the
devil's playthings-I'm the devil,
they do my work now)

but lifelines aren't straight

and ours meander through the
rivers and mountains

 and though parallel lines don't
cross

I've seen glimpses of you as the
sun flickers off the surface of your
line

parallel lines

and now our lines will never cross

they took buckets of water from
my river

(they emptied it-they had already

set the world on fire they
destroyedeverythingtheytouched)

and now that it's gone

and as we wade in the river of mud

we'll be a form of clean we never
could be before

and our lines will cross again.

to make a river

"take all your dreams and a few of
your sorrows, two stars and the
moon, and read this poem

to make a river."

when I looked up at the moon
searching for the sun (I didn't find
it-it was already after the time of
dreams) I saw these words in the
stars, as if they were waiting for
me

and in the daytime, I looked at the
sun and saw you

but the rain started to fall then, and
I was left alone without any dry
clothes to wear

and I walked home in the rain and
I felt that you wanted this

I swam in that river in my dreams

and when I woke up, I couldn't
remember that it was only a dream

and tomorrow, I will sleep and I'll
dream

and I will be in the land of
dreams and I won't leave

and I won't enter

and I will hear a voice saying to
me that you wanted this

and I swam in the sea two years
ago

and when I was under the water,
almost lifeless

I heard a voice crying to me that
you wanted this

i haven't seen the sun

It's been winter for ages now

I haven't seen the sun

standing in the forest with the trees
yet to wake

I felt myself turn into an ancient
memory that was born days ago

and the flames are hungry today

and now

you told me you could see the
smoke from years away

as the flame devoured me

and my anciently new history

and now that the smoke's cleared,

and as you sift through the wreckage once it's safe,

they told you I was the first to go

-I lost my will to fight long ago

and now the smoke's cleared

and now you can see why they called this forest "phoenix"

watch as it rises from the ashes

and I won'd be there

so burn it all to the ground.

and when the river starts flowing again

and once you know it's spring

think of me

and how I never saw the sun.

The sun will come out for the first time

feel the storm

my dear, take off that cloak of
sadness that weighs you down like
lead

every night, with your head up
against mine

I can tell you are holding back
tears

but I need to feel the storm

I need to know that I'm alive

(even though I never lived and
never will)

I wrote your name in the stars with
fire

(see how you can find your way
now?)

I made a lantern with dreams.

Icarus, come down from there!

I made a grave for him with his
feathers.

I buried him in his freedom.

abandoned houses

and at last this storm is over

and now you can breath easy

and as the smoke descends we can
see the truth:

that we never could
truly see

and now the worst is over

and now, stretch out your wings
and fly

　　(this storm has broken these
chains that bound you)

but my wings are broken now

and tell me, where is your soul
now?

　because now you're so broken it
can't be in the sky

　and those abandoned houses now

　　are where the broken ones go

　　　(after we've made ghosts of
them)

and when I find it, dear

　I'll paint it so gold

　　you won't be able to bear to
look at it

I'll give you Midas' touch

but just remember that all that
glisters is not always gold

　-remember that before you gild
your wings

and when you fall, dear Icarus,
remember

　I stood by you in those
abandoned houses

and I'll stand by you when you find
it abandoned

　　there, in a house up in the sky.

when you fly over

but I'll be there

waiting for the day
when you see my ashes in the
rubble

and you know I was always broken

so don't you cry, my dear

broken-hearted wings

Dear, don't stop talking

just pick yourself up and make
something with my ashes

while I sew your wings back
together

(this string is called Forgotten
Dreams; the needle Broken
Promises)

and don't you ever let that light in
your eyes fade

and you'll fly away with your
broken-hearted wings

while my nest burns

and the blackened ground will
mean nothing to you

shadows at the table

It's just shadows at this table
tonight

    and they sit and talk

      (talktalktalk their souls away)

    while we'll fly to the clouds

      and we'll do

but it's so dark outside

    and shadows can only come to
counter the night

but it's a once-in-a-lifetime thing

and I've seen it twice now

the sun was hidden for years

    but no one ever lied

    -you see, it's the darkness that
breeds trust

but then you came

    you weaved a web of lies with
your patchwork voice that
everyone heard but no one listened
to

and even the spiders got caught in
it

they starved as you watched

      as the hunter became the
hunted

    and when the shadows

      (you'll pretend they're eyes)

    came to your table to feast

you flew away to the clouds

never leave

and they talked

  I saw your ghost in the graveyard
last night

  and you did not

   and I whispered to you to get out
of the storm

   but you couldn't hear

  but dear, this is sacred ground

   consecrated by the blood of
society's victims

  we're all murderers here.

Dear, that was my soul you saw

 *I felt my wings break when I met
you*

 *(you were
soafraidsoafraiddon'tleaveme)*

but it's been gray ever since I met
you, almost like even nature
doesn't want me to leave

that was me that broke your wings

   I was
soafraidsoafraiddon'tleaveme

   so dear, just come in from that
storm

   before it takes your soul

      and you're left with nothing
but a cheap paper memory

            waiting for that fiery
monster Time to devour it

and now that I'm in from the storm

   I'll break your wings

                                          one day i'll soar

   so you can never leave.

Dear, you know I'm reckless

I swing on teeter-totters with my heart as the fulcrum

   waiting for gravity to let me go

each feather is one of my dreams

   they took me a lifetime to make

You know I'm reckless

   I walk on the sky with my eyes closed

(I'mnotafraidofheightsnotafraidnot afraid)

   you turned my world upside-down

and one day I'll soar

   I'll wear the sky on my shoulders

    just waiting for gravity to let me go

but my dear, promise me this tonight.

You know I'm reckless

   I spend my soul on birds

    buying them to let them out of their cages

   their freedom is my freedom

   when it rains sky-blue feathers and gilded butterflies

   when gravity lets go of me for the last time

   when I end up like Icarus on the broken-hearted ground

   you must not be afraid.

but I made these wings myself

and promise me that you'll take them

and when they come together of their own accord

and form a river

promise me you'll swim in it.

and I promise you one day I'll soar

one day

when gravity lets me go.

break down these walls

Let's break down these walls between us

and see this distance between us for the first time

let's fly in our dreams

and wake up in Germany 1989

and we'll watch the wall fall

Quickly, let's take these bricks

bring them back and build a future

close ourselves inside, never see out

we'll never look back

and though hindsight is 20/20

we have glasses made from our shattered hearts

and now we see so clearly where we're going

we see the fire ahead

we won't try to avoid it

it's so cold outside

so let's warm our souls in the flames

though they burn our soles

and let's burn down these walls

and warm our hearts in the
flames

and write our names in the sky

      I always thought that
Pisces looked like your name

and when it rains, we'll catch the
drops in our dreamcatcher

    we'll make this river from them

and as we lie together in it for the
last time

we'll watch as the walls fall.

when the ice cracks

Tell me when the ice cracks

   and I'll be there to catch you
when you fall

   (but it was me that dropped you
in the first place)

and we'll wish upon every star that
goes past

   as I tuck you into bed

and let your monster out of the closet

and the life is already leaving your eyes

And I was the master glassblower who took your broken heart

and made you these stars

and let's go down to the end of the earth

(it's only a mile away)

and the stars don't shine there

but we'll have your heart to light our way

and in the darkness of the daytime we'll arrive

and the specters in their horrifying beauty

will take everything you have from you

and leave only what you are

how much substance do you have?

and quick, give me your dreams

the sky is falling around us

but they'll keep it up there

they won't let it stop hugging the moon

and let the stars rain down

and I'll make a river of it

and watch it flow through our dreams

and we'll make a home at the end
of the earth

sitting here while the ice cracks.

                              and dry your tears, my dear

                                and I'll make a window with the
                              broken pieces of your heart

                                and all the stars to melt them
                              down

                              watch through the eclipse

eclipse the stars

                              And wipe the stardust off your
And it's the rain that brought them   pants
here

   the specters are here, they
smelled the blood

   and it's chaos out there   and the specters are here

   I'll watch   but it's those of your former self
                                     that hurt

      as they cut all your dreams

                                     as you sit in the shadows
   and the pavement's wet with
blood

and never forget the ghosts in your closet

or they'll come

and eclipse the stars

ever since you left

It's been raining ever since you left

as if even the weather can't be happy without you

the window decided to dream yesterday

.

it pretended it was sunny out

but my violin would only play in a minor scale

and my pen could only write in blood

and sign contracts with the devil.

It's been cloudy ever since you left

the sun won't show its face

And no one will cry

because it's been a ghost city for years

though its eyes paint truth

on canvases made of lies

though we've lived here forever in our dreams

and I painted a Van Gogh

with the brushes made by cardboard cutouts

and let's go watch it from the clouds

so let's burn it all down, my dear

nothing to bring us down

watch the fire burn down this city I built of

except for life.

bricks made of lies

and blood to hold it together

and let's burn it all down, my dear

rebuild it from the ashes

and see what lies it'll tell

rainy nights

It's a rainy night in the City of
Lights

There's no one outside save for
you

  but the city's never felt so
crowded.

It's an invisible rainy Monday as I
watch the cars go by

  I'm about to say something to you

  but then I remember.

I go back to watching the phantom
cars that only I can see.

I walk down the streets and give
them each a name-

  La pleine lune vide, this one

  Ma joie perdue, the next

The street signs look back at me
with empty eyes where I see my
reflection trying to break free.

And then the sun came out, and I
felt my breath leave me slowly

  I still can't breathe right

and before the last puddle
vanished, I looked into it

it said Erised around it

  and I saw a cloudy sky

  and you alongside me

  a figure only I can see.

i will haunt you forever.

i will haunt you forever

I.

thrown in a river

told them he couldn't swim

they laughed.

the current knew no mercy

nothing but *kill and let live*

it was nothing but a mercenary,

    though it wasn't gold that paid
the fee

a life for a life is what nature
demanded

II.

you bigots

    you that kill with your mouths

when will you ever learn?

      hate is nothing

   but the embodiment of your
fears

    your phobias

i will haunt you forever

to love

III.

   let me define a word for you now

it will haunt you forever.

phobia

IV.

it means senseless fear

they laughed

     it took his life

that one sound

and it takes your souls

echoed throughout the forest that night

   your hearts

when no other sound existed

   your minds

   your love

i could have sworn it was the sound of crying

   unless you learn to surrender it

and not laughter.

tonight i heard someone laugh

V.

now it haunts me forever

and i cried.

the memory

the laughter was the
same as what i heard that night

an innocent life

they are still afraid

and a guilty death

of love

though the guilt was not his

but theirs.

i will haunt you forever.

it is theirs to live with forever

their memory

has nothing to see

for better or for worse

except for that river

that mercenary

i will haunt you forever

that would not kill

for gold

VI.

i will haunt you forever.

it will be for worse

that is my prophecy

VII.

this is society's guilt too

the blood is on their hands

i have seen the path of hatred

they are that river

a soul filled with hatred

they do not kill for gold

i will haunt them forever

yet they still take the gold that
is not offered to them.

.

and even though they were
caught red-handed

we flew on angels' wings

they walk away as if they had
never known guilt

the sky was gilded

like angels' wings that night.

we stitched the wings

to our backs

and as they do

with the string of friendship

a voice echoes throughout the
forest,

and flew away into the dark night.

does nothing but give

birth to something new.

we flew away on angels' wings.

and i never knew

that the end

could be the beginning

of so much.

the sky was gilded

like angels' wings.

we put those wings on our backs

-a new backpack bought for school-

but here we are

the beginning of the end

and we flew away on angels' wings

or the end

of the beginning?

but all beginnings

are ends in disguise

and the end

to the bottom.

20000 feet up

breathing is a swear word.

this climb has taken my

    breath, my shoes are

    in tatters just like my

    broken spirit.

maybe that's why the bottom

    of a shoe is a soul.

i never knew that forever

    was how long it was to the
top

and now it is never

and from up here, my soul

    is colder than the snow.

and from up here, it looks like
never

    to the bottom.

and from up here, it looks like

    everything is made

  of tiny sparks

    of life hope souls snow breath

and from up here, the smell of
airplanes

  is as sweet as roses.

20,000 feet to get here

when you asked,

infinite feet to get down.

"want to climb for forever?"

but who would ever want to?

i thought you meant

a whole day.

my lungs are in tatters

but that day

    just like the soles of your
shoes

became forever

quickly, and now

and my heart is shattered

    just like the sky next to you.

we have been gone forever,

and if we go down

and it has never been clearer to me

    that forever is just a
mountain climb away

none of our friends

will know us anymore.

so let's just stay.

.

and so we start the descent to
never

     that we know we will
never finish

so we won't even try.

a track of forever

there was a smoldering piece of us.
it

fell from your cheeks in the form
of

and breathing is a swear word

that which other people call tears,
but

i knew better: i saw our faces
squashed together in the form

and it's my favorite word.

of love reflected in its watery fury.

it burned a track of forever in your cheeks, and

if you look closely in the mirror now,

you might be able to see the headlights of the

train that other people call

forgetfulness

shining down that track of forever that we

burned into your cheeks.

and they called it a river in that

town halfway across the world,

when they saw the sunlight

reflected off those cheeks.

but we knew better, for, even

though it was a river, the sunlight

did not make your cheeks shine like

that:

the river did that by itself. the waters of

hope caressed its trench that other people

call a river.

i could see the pieces of sunlight in the sky

as you talked, and it seemed to me like

the sunlight was coming out of your

mouth as words, and some magic

in the air, leftover from when the

tears evaporated from your cheeks,

turned them into sunlight.

and they flew away on gilded wings, and

they made themselves nests in the night sky,

to light up our way as we kept the day

alive with our words.

what if/forest fires

What if i could be

a star? if i could

light up the night

sky and go on

shining after time

caught me in its

10-gallon glass jar?

What if i could be

the sun? if i could

light up the day, even

when i'm 9 million miles

away they would see me.

and i could radiate heat

like a forest fire burning

10 thousand years down

as if it was no more than

a word. and they felt

its heat 10 thousand years

from here. and they said in

a town halfway across the

world that it was no more

than the sunset, but in

that place 10 thousand

years away from there,

the sun was smiling from

its midday chair.

what if i could fly

instead of walking? i

tried that today, but

just like Icarus, my

wings made of

hope were too close to

that 10 thousand day old

fire, and i fell

to the grass.

and the sky cried this morning,

for the 10 thousand years that

the heat destroyed. and this

morning, i couldn't tell the
difference

between the tears and the dew,

so i pretended that they were all
just

little drops of hope that the day

gave to me to make something out
of.

and i took them in my hands made
of

fire, and crafted them into a

river to flow into other peoples'

dreams.

and people praised that river, they

said it looked like the

sky. and they said "it figures it

was made with hands of fire."

everyone knows you need fire

to make something new.

and that river looked just like
dreams

today, and it held up the sky

with its waterfall that went up
instead

of down. and they said in that town

halfway across the world that it

was really holding hands with

the sky.

everyone knows that dreams walk

hand-in-hand with the sky.

saltwater taught me cuts i didn't
even know i had.

the sky cried that saturday,

each mile you drove on was a mile
i had spent my life wishing i would
never see.

i guess that goes to show, never
spend your life wishing on
airplanes when you're

too blind to tell they're not
shooting stars.

the sky cried that saturday

the saltwater changed that day's
name to "never"

the sky cried that saturday

 glass meets water again and again

with each new tear comes another
painful memory, a

day that i tried to forget

but each time the sky cried it
opened up another wound, the

the sky cried that saturday

you pulled over and wiped the
tears from my eyes, the tears i
dismissed as rain

that lie was more transparent than
glass

my window was closed.

that hug you gave me was an
eternity, but

that open door betrayed me, the

falling told me the truth i was
hoping i could deny.

dreams will always tell you their
real name.

the sky cried that saturday

each mile you drove away was a
mile i had spent my life wishing i
would never see

the fading tail lights looked just
like the airplanes i had spend my
life wishing on, pretending

they were shooting stars.

cemetery of forgotten souls

this is the cemetery of forgotten
souls.

welcome, all you breathing dead

it is dark today, the wind's soul is
heavy now.

do you see its shadow there? that is
the shadow

of the earth, of a forgotten forever.

this is the cemetery of forgotten souls.

are you confused? you will find no bodies

under these tombstones, these names refuse to be

found in the obituary pages.

this is the cemetery of forgotten souls.

did you hear that clock strike? it just struck never.

that is the time when these souls wake.

this is the cemetery of forgotten souls.

look, there is the shadow of the wind. welcome it:

it lives here, that is why mortals do not know its name.

this is the cemetery of forgotten souls.

goodbye, do not forget us.

oh? what's that? you can't get out?

i forgot to tell you: only the hopeful can leave.

what's that? you're not?

then welcome to the cemetery of forgotten souls.

it rained last night

It rained last night.
The water washed away
everything but us, and when you splashed
in the puddles i could have sworn
i heard some forgotten voice that i
remember now crying out
love and peace and forgiveness.

It rained last night.
The pitter-patter on our roof
blocked all the sounds out but us.

There we were,
talking the night away as if
nothing mattered but us. But
time would not stop for us, day
came too soon, but then we
realized
the rain had washed everything
away but us, and we went outside
and splashed in the puddles.
The water wouldn't move, even
though we taught it the weight of
our feet
in the early morning. And i could
have sworn i heard some voice cry
out
not to forget hir. But i have
forgotten hir already.

It rained last night.
The sweet scent blocked out
everything but peace. And you
asked me with fear in your voice,
"do you hear those sirens?" But i
just smiled and we kept on talking
as if nothing mattered but us.

And then the sun rose. And yes, i
heard those sirens. But last night,
nothing mattered but us.
And no, i don't know what they
were for, but the rain washed away
everything
but us. And no, don't worry, the
rain washed away those sirens too.

It rained last night.

The rain washed away everything
but us. And you asked me, "did it
wash away hope too?" And i just
put my arm
around you, and we kept talking,
as if nothing mattered but us.

And yes, it washed away hope too,
but hope is overrated, we have
each other. And that's all we need.
Sometimes, i think the doctors got
the baskets switched up when we
were born. And instead of hope,
we got these names. And now that
the rain washed away everything
but us, hope can know its true
name again.

And its true name is us.

Made in the USA
Lexington, KY
11 January 2015